presented to:

by:

snapshots of Heaven

Joyce Vollmer Brown

illustrated by

Gwendolyn Babbitt

COUNTRYMAN

Published by J. Countryman, a division of Thomas Nelson, Inc.,

Nashville, Tennessee 37214.

Project Editor: Terri Gibbs

Designed by Left Coast Design Inc. Portland, Oregon.

ISBN: 08499-5654-4

Printed in the United States of America

www.jcountryman.com

To David, Ryan, and Phil:
May the circle be unbroken
on that glorious shore.

In Heaven . . . .

In heaven...

We'll arm wrestle with Samson, go fishing with
Peter, ask Noah how he got all the animals
into the ark, hear what Daniel was thinking
as he looked at those lions, and listen to
Mary's stories about Jesus' childhood.

In heaven...
we'll swap jokes
with Chuck
Swindoll, sing
songs with
Steve Green,
play catch
with Orel
Hershiser,
and take
hikes with
Joni Eareckson
Tada.

In heaven...

We'll be reunited with dear friends and
family members who have died.
We'll get to know countless generations of our
ancestors.
We'll meet people whose lives we touched in
ways we never knew.
And we'll never run out of things to talk about.

In heaven...

we'll be surrounded by heroes—the finest,

brightest, bravest, most noble people from

all over the world throughout all of time.

And we'll never run out of things to talk about.

In heaven...

We'll get to know angels who were on hand
when the earth was created, angels who sang
to the shepherds that first Christmas, and
angels who watched over us on earth.

In heaven...

Angels will tell us how they learned from us!

(Ephesians 3:10)

14

In heaven...

There will only be hellos—no good-byes.
There won't be any broken hearts or broken homes.
Love will never die.

In heaven...

Our hearts will always be wide open;

we'll have nothing to hide because all of our

guilt will be gone.

In heaven...
we'll share
everything
we have
because
we'll never
worry about
not having
enough.

In heaven...

No one will ever be angry, rude, or unkind.
Everyone will always be incredibly nice.

In heaven...

No one will have a big ego. Everyone will be
poor in spirit—amazed by the grace that
brought them there.

In heaven...

Instead of competing against one
another, we'll cheer for each
other.

We'll never feel awkward or
dumb because no one will ever
look down on us.

Gwendolyn
Babbitt
@1997

In heaven...

We will still be individuals with
unique appearances, talents,
and personalities.

We'll not only be ourselves, but all
that God meant us to be.

In heaven...
we'll be different
without having
differences.

There won't

be any

Democrats

or Republicans,

conservatives

or liberals, Baptists or Lutherans.

No prejudice or discrimination, arguments or

disagreements.

There will be perfect harmony because everyone will have one mind (the mind of Christ) and one goal (to glorify God).

In heaven...

There won't be any strangers.

Everyone will be part of one HUGE, loving family.

In heaven...

We'll love those we loved on earth a thousand times more, and we'll love thousands of others as well.

In heaven...

We'll accept each other totally—just as we
are—because we'll all be perfect.
No one will have any faults or flaws!

In heaven...

We'll be surrounded by people with unlimited
capacity to love.

In heaven...

There won't be any locked doors or security alarms.

In heaven...

There will be no need for cameras or scrapbooks.

We won't need to capture wonderful moments and sights because every day will be a magnificent memory in the making, and beyond each turn will be a scene more breathtaking than the last.

In heaven...

There won't be any bills in the mailbox.

There won't be any commercials, salespeople, or phone solicitors because everything will be free!

In heaven...

Instead of the government taking more and more and more,
the government will give and give and give.

In heaven...

There won't be any sleazy campaigns or
corrupt politicians.

The government will be flawless—with officials
appointed by God.

In heaven...

Retarded children will have mental abilities
greater than earthly geniuses.
The blind will see, the deaf will sing, the
crippled will dance, and the poor will wear
fine clothes and live in luxury.

In heaven...

People who were "nobodies" on earth
will be put in charge of whole cities.

In heaven...

God will give bigger rewards to Christians with great attitudes than those with great achievements.

He'll reward the faithful more than the successful.

In heaven...

We'll be treated royally wherever we go.

We'll never be put on hold or have to wait

in long lines.

We'll be

known by

name—

not an I.D.

number.

In heaven...

We'll believe everything we hear.

There won't be any slanted news,

distorted facts, or exaggerated stories.

No deceptions or lies. Truth will reign.

In heaven...

The news will always be something to

celebrate.

There won't be a single sad or disturbing

story.

In heaven...

We'll never have to do anything we don't want to, and we'll never run out of things we want to do!

In heaven...

We'll not only be adopted into God's family,

but into His business as well.

It will be such a privilege to have a hand

in something so big and so important.

In heaven...

Everyone will have work they love to do.

Work will never be boring, stressful, unfulfilling, or unappreciated.

Success will be guaranteed because we'll never fail or make mistakes.

34

In heaven...

Many people will
have to find
new vocations.
There won't be
a need for
doctors,
nurses,
pharmacists,
dentists, lawyers, social workers,
beauticians, psychiatrists, insurance agents,
soldiers, bankers, undertakers, tax collectors,
police, or repairmen.

In heaven...

we'll be like

children in

all the good

ways:

innocent,

carefree,

open, and

fun-loving.

We'll trust

everyone,

be eager to learn,

and be filled with wonder.

In heaven...

we will no longer need faith to believe

because we'll see and know.

In heaven...

We won't pray any more.

We'll talk to God face to face.

We won't have any sins to confess or needs to ask for.

We will praise and thank God without ceasing.

In heaven...

There won't be any churches or temples.
Every inch of heaven will be holy and pure
and filled with God's presence.

In heaven...

Wherever we go, we'll be home. We'll never wish we were somewhere else, doing something else, or with someone else.

In heaven...

There will only be two kinds of tears—
tears of laughter and tears of joy.

We will never be

angry,

lonely,

frustrated,

frightened,

discouraged,

overwhelmed,

dissatisfied,

or depressed.

In heaven...

We'll have such a fantastic time that decades, even centuries will fly by.

In heaven...

It won't be hard to be good. The Tempter won't be around to trip us up.

In heaven...

We won't need cars, trains, or planes.

We'll move throughout the galaxy in an instant.

If something gets in our way, we'll just go

through it!

43

In heaven...

We'll know life without bounds—with no restrictions from budgets, health, or physical abilities.

No speed limits, time limits, or red tape.

No limits to love, patience, or understanding. We'll be free from fear, doubt, and sin— free to be all we were created to be.

In heaven...

Nothing will seem impossible.
Nothing will ever go wrong because God's will,
will always be done.

In heaven...

We won't say, "How are you?" in greeting
because the answer will always be the
same:

"Fantastic!" or "Incredible!" or
"Unbelievable!"

In heaven...

No one will warn us to "Be careful" because

there won't be any dangers.

In heaven...

We won't say, "I wish . . ." because every
longing we've ever had will be satisfied.
We'll be totally content.

In heaven...

We won't say, "If only . . ." because we won't
have any regrets.

In heaven...

We won't say, "What if . . ." There will be
nothing to worry about because we won't
be able to lose any blessings.

In heaven...

We'll never describe anything by saying, "It was good while it lasted" because everything good will last forever.

In heaven...

If we ask someone, "What's new?" we'll sit
and listen for hours—maybe even days.
There will always be countless new delights
and discoveries to share.

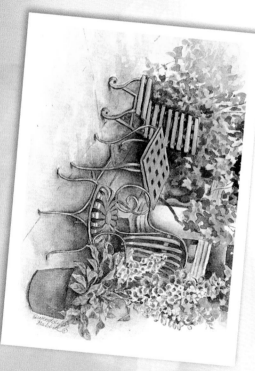

In heaven...

We won't use the word "too."

The weather will never be too hot or too cold.

No distance will be too great. No place will be too crowded.

We'll never have too much on our mind or too many things to do.

Everything will always be just right.

In heaven...

We'll say "Hallelujah!" "Hosanna!" "Praise God!"
and "Thank You, Jesus!" over and over.

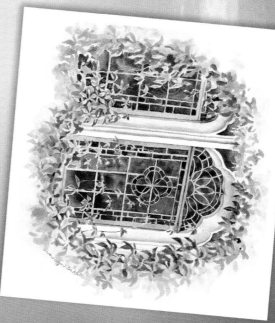

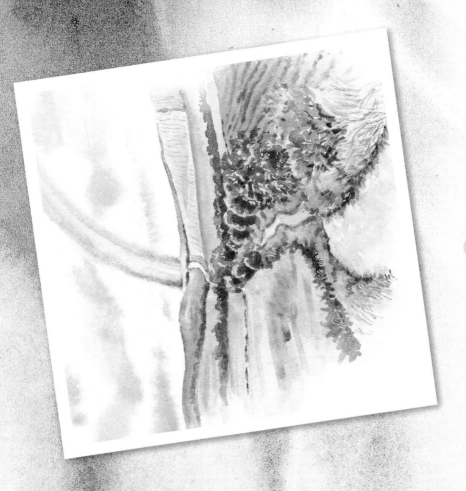

In heaven...

We won't spoil things like we did on earth.

The air will stay fresh and clean.

Rivers will sparkle.

No garbage will mar the beauty of the landscape.

In heaven...

Memories of earth's greatest glories will seem drab and paltry.

Diamond-capped waves,
crimson sunsets,
star-studded skies,
ice-crystal
covered trees
sparkling in the sun—
will be faint shadows
of the breathtaking
beauty surrounding us.

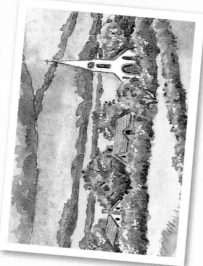

In heaven...

we'll live in

a new

Jerusalem

where

everything

will be

bigger,

brighter, and better

than anything we've ever imagined.

It will be 1,500 miles long, 1,500 miles wide, and

1,500 miles high (big enough so millions of

redeemed will have plenty of room).

57

In heaven...

The city's walls will be covered with jewels of many colors and have gates cut into giant pearls. (We'll be able to leave the city through these gates and travel throughout the universe.)

Its shining streets will be made of transparent gold.

God's throne will be in the center of the city. Behind the throne a beautiful rainbow will remind us of His loving grace.

In heaven...

Even though Jerusalem won't be lit by the sun or moon, we won't need any candles or lights because the whole city will be filled with warm, glowing light—from the glory of God.

The heavenly city will be a city of life.
The river of the water of life, clear as crystal,
will flow from the throne down the main street
of the city.

Trees of life will grow on either side of it. Each
tree will be like a fruit-of-the-month club,
bearing a different kind of crop each month.

The curse and all of its negative effects will
be removed.

There will be lush, gorgeous vegetation (like the
Garden of Eden).

Fruit won't decay. Flowers won't wither. Trees and
plants will flourish—undamaged by insects,
unstunted by disease, uncrowded by weeds.

In heaven...

We'll each have a wonderful home
custom built to suit us, lavishly
decorated to reflect our tastes,
lovingly prepared with everything
we need to be happy and
comfortable.

60

In heaven...

Nothing will break, fade,
wear out, or decay.

Everything will always be
fresh and new.

In heaven...

Nothing will
ever smell bad.

In heaven...

Even the animals will live peacefully.

Wolves and lambs, calves and lions,

bears and snakes will live side by side.

In heaven...

Everything will be pure and unadulterated.

All of our thoughts will be holy.

Our love will be completely unselfish,

our motives unmixed,

our behavior faultless,

our worship perfect,

and our joy absolute.

In heaven...

It will always be spring,

always be morning,

always the beginning

—never the end.

In heaven...

Every day will be new and different.

There will be never-ending variety.

Our wonder will never wear off.

In heaven...

One day will be better than a thousand
on earth, and we'll have thousands of
thousands of days times thousands of
thousands of thousands . . .

In heaven...

Storehouses of blessings are ready and
waiting for us.

In heaven...

As God's adopted children we'll receive an inheritance of untold wealth, countless rewards for every tiny act of obedience and service we ever performed, and an endless shower of gifts to demonstrate His never-ending love.

In heaven...

We'll finally understand how wide and long
and high and deep God's love for us is.

In heaven...

We'll never be anxious or impatient for the
future because our attention will be
totally captivated by unimaginable joy
and miraculous wonders of the present.

In heaven...

Every day will be like our birthday, Valentine's
Day, and Christmas
combined.

Life will be so exciting
that we'll feel like
kids who don't want
to go to bed
because they're
afraid of missing
something.

And we'll never have
to, since we won't
need to sleep.

In heaven...

There won't be any cosmetic counters; every woman will be gorgeous naturally.

In heaven...

There won't be any wrinkled faces, gray hair, or bald heads; no false teeth or bifocals, no stooped shoulders, arthritic joints, or fading memories. Everyone will be in their prime of life forever.

In heaven...

We'll experience wonders no eyes have ever seen, no ears have ever heard, no hearts have even hoped for.

Senses we have now will be heightened, and we'll have new senses as well.

In heaven...

we'll probably know one another
instantly just as
Peter, James,
and John
knew Moses
and Elijah
on the mountaintop.

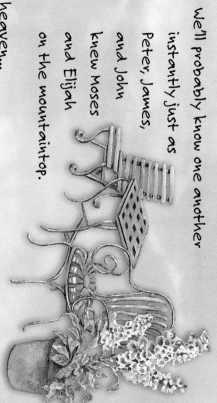

In heaven...

we'll have unimaginable abilities.
we may be telepathic and read each other's
minds. (That will be OK since we won't have
any unkind or impure thoughts.)

In heaven...
We won't wish we could change a single thing about ourselves!

Our bodies, personalities, characters, thoughts, and actions will all be perfect.

In heaven...
We will talk and act and think and love—like Christ.

In heaven...

we'll never stop
learning and
growing. we'll
develop our
gifts and
abilities
and
discover

talents we never knew we had.
we'll accomplish things we dreamed of,
but didn't have the time or opportunity
to do on earth.

In heaven...

Like a blushing bride whose eyes focus on her beloved rather than her own beauty, we will hardly notice our own glory.

All eyes will be fixed upon God. Every look will be filled with love, every heart will be filled with wonder.

In heaven...

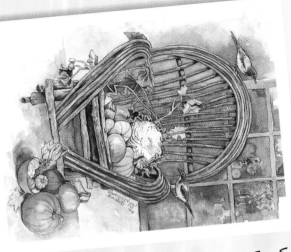

We'll be crowned
with majesty and
honor. Like kings
and queens, we'll
rule the earth
with Christ and
judge angels.
Yet we'll cast our
crowns at Jesus'
feet without
hesitating.

In heaven...

Although our lives will be filled with
unlimited blessings, none will compare
with the joy of walking and talking with
Jesus and knowing God intimately—the
way He has always known us.

There won't be any veil between us or any
door we must knock on.

We won't have to wait for Him to agree
to receive us.

He will always welcome us, always be
delighted to spend time with us.

In heaven...

we'll feel more at home than we ever did
on earth because we'll be with our
Father.

we'll see how tenderly He loves us each
time we look in His eyes.

Our hearts will thrill as He tells us how
proud He is of us.

He'll protect us from harm and keep all evil
from us.

He'll patiently teach us, answer our
questions, and gently mold our spirit
and character to make us more like
Him.

©Brenda Lynn Blackard

In heaven...

We'll lose ourselves and our self-centered focus.

Our thoughts will be consumed with God's awesome glory, power, and love.

In heaven...

we'll worship

effortlessly without

distractions,

openly without

self-consciousness,

confidently with no insecurity about

where we stand,

completely with no guilt holding us back,

spontaneously and continuously with

an overflowing heart.

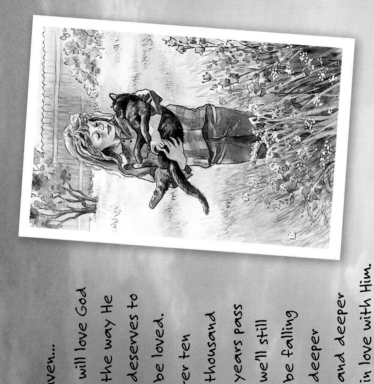

In heaven...

We will love God
the way He
deserves to
be loved.

After ten

thousand

years pass

we'll still

be falling

deeper

and deeper

in love with Him.

In heaven...

A never-ending "welcome home" party is
  waiting for our arrival.

Our heavenly Father will come to greet us
  with open, loving arms.

Jesus, our older brother, will bring us a robe
  and a crown.

And our hearts will be overcome with joy and
  relief to finally be home to stay.

Afterword

Looking forward to an eternal home in heaven transforms life here and now. Remembering the joy that awaits us helps us endure difficult times. Realizing how much God loves us fills our hearts with love and gratitude. Knowing He uses events in our lives to prepare us for heaven gives them meaning. Viewing life with an eternal perspective gives it purpose because our acts of service will one day be rewarded many times over.

Everyone is invited to come to heaven. But we must respond and accept the invitation. Only those whose names are in the reservation book will be admitted. (Revelation 21:27 says:

"Nothing impure will ever enter (Heaven), nor will anyone who does what is shameful or deceitful, but only those whose names are written in the Lamb's book of life."

If you're not sure your name is in that book, keep reading to learn how you can find that assurance.

God loves you and created you so He could have a personal relationship with you. Jesus said: "For God so loved the world that he gave his one and only Son, that whoever believes in him shall not perish but have eternal life" (John 3:16).

Everyone has sinned. Our sin keeps us from

being close to Him. "For all have sinned, and fall short of the glory of God . . ." (Revelation 3:23).

"But your iniquities (sins) have separated you from your God; your sins have hidden his face from you, so that he will not hear" (Isaiah 59:2).

Sin has a penalty. "For the wages of sin is death, but the gift of God is eternal life in Christ Jesus our Lord" (Romans 6:23).

Christ paid that penalty. "But God demonstrates his own love for us in this: while we were still sinners, Christ died for us" (Romans 5:8).

Salvation is a free gift. "For it is by grace you have been saved, through faith—and this not from yourselves, it is the gift of God—not by works, so that no one can boast" (Ephesians 2:8-9).

Jesus invites us to know Him. "Here I am! I stand at the door and knock. If anyone hears my voice and opens the door, I will come in and eat with him, and he with me" (Revelation 3:20).

We must respond. "To all who received him, to those who believed in his name, he gave the right to become children of God . . ." (John 1:12). To accept Christ's offer of salvation and invitation to Heaven you must: (1) turn to God from your own way of living; (2) depend on Christ's death and resurrection to provide God's forgiveness; (3) allow God to begin to direct your life.

To begin a lifelong relationship with God that will last for all of eternity, pray a simple prayer like this: "God, I know my sins have come between us. I thank you for sending Jesus to die in my place. I trust in Jesus as my personal Savior. Please forgive me for my sins and come into my life and show me the way You want me to live. Thank you for giving me eternal life. Amen."